LONDON UNDERGROUND IN COLOUR

JOHN GLOVER

First published 1997

ISBN 0 7110 2530 4

Published by Ian Allan Publishing

an imprint of Ian Allan Ltd, Terminal House,
Station Approach, Shepperton, Surrey TW17 8AS.
Printed by Ian Allan Printing Ltd at its works at
Coombelands in Runnymede, England.

Code: 9708/C

Introduction

London Underground carries about 2.5 million passengers every weekday, with the heaviest traffic on the District and Northern Lines. These are followed, in order, by the Central, Piccadilly and Victoria Lines. The busiest section of the Underground in the morning peak is from Liverpool Street to Bank, with over 40,000 passengers being carried in the 3hr period. The busiest Underground station is Victoria, with 66 million passenger entries and exits, plus 18 million interchanges, every year.

Such statistics, culled from a report by London Transport Marketing, show that London Underground is a large business by anybody's standards. Yet it is by no means the busiest Metro system in the world. Passenger usage in London is only a quarter of that in Moscow.

Let us examine what the Underground railways of London have needed to achieve. First, the demand for travel must be there. London is an old, established city, in being long before the railways arrived. The dispersal of the main line stations around the edge of the central area and the need for cheap and effective transport was enough. It resulted in the construction of the Metropolitan and the Metropolitan District Railways, both with steam traction, from the 1860s.

But cut and cover construction is tremendously disruptive. Enter the tube railway, but this had to await some technical advances. These included the ability to bore tunnels, the development of electric traction and multiple unit control, and passenger access to deep level by lifts (or, later, escalators). Other essential elements included ventilation and drainage requirements. The tube as we know it is essentially a 20th-century invention.

Next came system expansion. By the end of the Edwardian era, the in-town construction of most of the tube lines was largely complete. Subsequent expansion took place in the interwar period, with the new suburban extensions and in some cases the takeover of main line railway branches, albeit that the Central Line work was not completed until after the war and that for the Northern Line never was. The only new post-1945 lines are the Victoria Line in total, the Heathrow additions to the Piccadilly, and the building of the Jubilee from Baker Street southwards.

How has the Underground fared, as a business? Historical comparisons are difficult, since the system size has been far from constant over the years. There have always been fluctuations in passenger volumes, since these tend to follow Britain's (and particularly London's) economic fortunes. However, more recent figures give the highest totals, if for no other reason than that the system is now at its greatest extent ever. Present expectations are that passenger numbers will expand further in future years; already London Underground carries more passengers every year than the whole of the main line railway system.

When it comes to productive efficiency, staff numbers have shown a continuous decline. But should the operation be regarded only as a business? The formal function of London Transport is to meet the transport needs of Greater London (London Regional Transport Act 1984, Section 2).

Finally, in a historical context anyway, the Underground has had an enviable reputation for architectural and design elegance. Much remains more or less unaltered today, while the Jubilee Line Extension may well offer some very different and exciting new vistas. Daylight penetrating deep-level tube platforms? Well, perhaps. While the design aspect primarily concerns buildings and furnishings, the trains themselves have also evolved over time.

It may be concluded that the Underground's time of greatest success varies according to the matters being considered. Perhaps the best is yet to come? The need is to tap investment funding so that the system can be both renewed and expanded. If the Underground organisation has to be restructured in order to achieve this, then so be it.

There is no shortage of projects, which include the Chelsea-Hackney line as well as light-rail type schemes. Croydon Tramlink and the DLR Lewisham Extension are already progressing. Is there more scope for the Underground south of the Thames through a mix of new construction and the taking over of some Railtrack lines? What relatively low-cost options are

---

Front cover: By December 1996, this A stock train had received the present Underground corporate livery. It is seen passing Kilburn at the head of a train for Aldgate on the outer, non-platformed, Metropolitan Line tracks. This is one of the few instances in Britain where the slow lines with all-stations trains (here the Jubilee) are placed in between the fast lines. Aldgate, which used to see Metropolitan Line trains during peak hours only, now has a much more extensive service pattern. *John Glover*

Back cover: A four-car train of 1938 stock survives in its final Underground form and was used at the Northern Line centenary celebrations in November 1990. The train provided a shuttle service to and from Morden depot, from which it is seen arriving during the day. The window surrounds are painted cream, as in earlier livery styles. This train is owned by the LT Museum. *John Glover*

Previous page: Eric Aumonier's symbolic Rapid Transit archer at East Finchley points towards central London in a position he has now maintained for over half a century. Whether his intended route is via the never completed tube link to Finsbury Park and Moorgate, or via Archway, is not revealed. For those bound for Northern City branch destinations, the present route offers no speed advantage to that of the LNER line in the interwar period. This picture was taken in September 1990. *John Glover*

available, such as the East London Line extensions at both the northern and the southern ends, and how should these be taken forward? Is the Underground really the right operator for this, or should it be a Train Operating Company? More generally, where should the dividing lines be between light rail, Underground and main line railway operation?

Some projects involve primarily the main line railways, notably the Channel Tunnel Rail Link, with its stations at Stratford and St Pancras; Thameslink 2000 and CrossRail. All of these are likely to have major impacts on Underground patronage and some may be interdependent. There is, for instance, little point in planning to deposit trainloads of international passengers at King's Cross if they cannot disperse using the local transport system.

Sustainable mobility is one of today's objectives. The Underground is an electrically-powered mass mover of passengers, which does not impact on road use in the confined space of a developed and densely occupied city. If that is not a highly desirable form of sustainable mobility, what is?

This book has more modest objectives than to provide the answers to these questions, though they need to be asked. It examines, over the last quarter century, some of the visible aspects of London Underground and the Docklands Light Railway; in particular the trains, the accommodation they offer and the stations. How does the public rate what it sees, and is it satisfied? There are no conclusions; these are matters for the reader.

My thanks to Brian Morrison, Martin Higginson and GEC Alsthom for their help with providing illustrations.

John Glover   *April 1997*
Worcester Park
Surrey

Right:
In October 1987, a train of 1973 stock catches the evening light as it approaches South Ealing from Northfields, which station can be seen in the background. Leicester Square to Covent Garden, at 0.26km, may be the shortest inter-station distance on London Underground, but the 0.48km seen here is decidedly at the shorter end of the spectrum. In reality, as much depends on the relative position of station entrances as on the location of the centre of the platforms. The four-track layout here is deceptive. While both westbound tracks here (on the left of the picture) are used, that on the far right sees test running only and has no regular passenger use. *John Glover*

East Acton eastbound platform is seen here in April 1995 as a train of 1992 stock with DM No 91279 in the lead arrives. This 1920 station was built to accommodate the westwards extension of the Central London Railway to Ealing Broadway. The wooden shelter is more reminiscent of main line railway construction than that of the Underground companies, but that is perhaps an understandable result of the Great Western Railway's interest in its construction. *John Glover*

The London & South Western Railway likewise extended eastwards from Richmond to beyond Ravenscourt Park, at which point the line turned north to a station at Grove Road and then made a junction with the Hammersmith & City Railway. The connection was removed totally in 1932 in conjunction with the four-tracking of the line west of Hammersmith (District and Piccadilly). Its remains are seen here in a view looking westwards in March 1995, with a Dagenham East-bound train of D stock approaching. Both Piccadilly Line tracks and the westbound District (with train) are on the far side of the disused formation. *John Glover*

The East London Line has seen a variety of rolling stock over the years, often the oldest in the fleet at the time. Part of the reason for this is the limited stock requirement; a maximum of five four-car trains has been adequate in most recent timetables. The line is presently undergoing an extended closure, during which the Brunel tunnels under the Thames are being renewed and the new Canada Water JLE interchange station constructed. In happier days, A60 stock DM No 5065 is seen in a new Underground experimental livery at Surrey Quays on a New Cross train in June 1990. *John Glover*

Above:
Morden, the southern tip of the Northern Line, is approached in tunnel from East Finchley or Golders Green. The last section is in cut and cover construction. This May 1990 view of the five-platform (but only three-tracked) station was taken from above the tunnel mouth. In each platform can be seen a train of 1959 stock: that on the left is for High Barnet via Charing Cross, the centre for Edgware via Charing Cross, right for Hampstead via Bank. No wonder Northern Line operation is complex! *John Glover*

Right:
Morden station, the new terminus of the reconstructed and extended City & South London Railway, was opened on 13 September 1926. This Underground symbol is contained in the façade above the station entrance from the street and bus station outside. It catches the weak morning sunlight in this December 1996 view. *John Glover*

7

The early City & South London Railway stations of 1890 were all equipped with hydraulic lifts, with a dome to house the winding gear. The listed Kennington is the only one to retain the dome, although it is no longer used for this purpose. The station itself was extensively reconstructed below ground to accommodate the extension from Charing Cross in 1926, as well as the rebuilding of the C&SLR. This picture was taken in December 1996.
John Glover

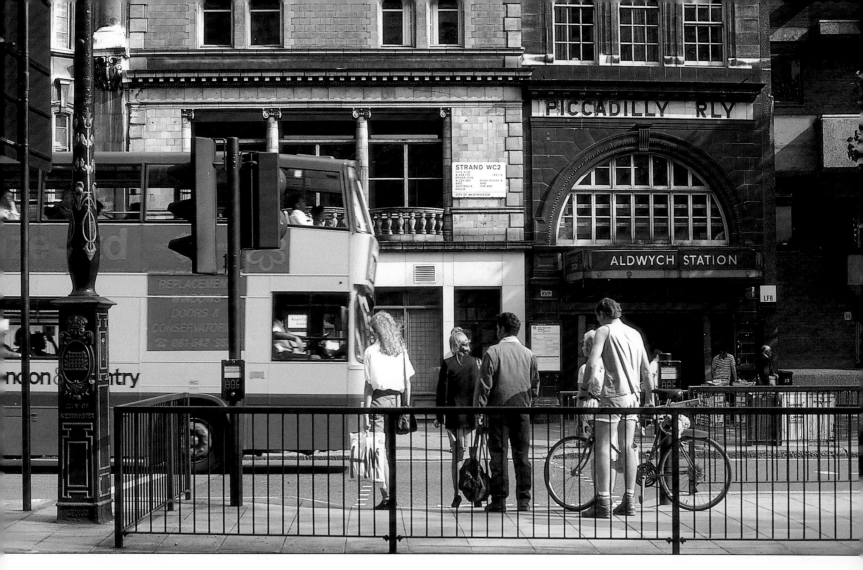

More typical of early tube surface building architecture were the 'oxblood' station entrances of Leslie Green. Originally over 50 were built, but their numbers diminished with the substitution of escalators for lifts. Either the point where the escalator reached the platform access would be different, or the surface building had to move. Aldwych station in this 1994 picture has only months left, the Piccadilly Line branch from Holborn closing on 1 October of that year. Passing the station is a London & Country bus on Route 176. This is not a railway replacement service, though it does indeed run between the same two points as part of a longer route. *Martin Higginson*

Although an early addition to the underground railway network in 1900, the Waterloo & City Line was the result of the London & South Western Railway's wish to give its passengers access to the City from Waterloo. This mirrored the Great Western's interest in the Metropolitan Railway from Paddington Bishop's Road nearly 40 years earlier, for similar reasons. However, unlike the Metropolitan, the Waterloo & City became part of the Southern Railway and later Network SouthEast. A train of the English Electric 1940-built Class 487 stock is seen at Bank in June 1991, about to depart for Waterloo. *Brian Morrison*

Times change, and the new trains for 'the Drain' after 50 years of the Class 487s were clones of the 1992 stock, then being built by ADtranz for the Central Line. On 1 April 1994, the Waterloo & City was transferred to the custody of London Underground. Whether or not LU were pleased at the acquisition of a 2.37km line with two stations only and a very highly peaked patronage, they were too polite to say. Here, three months after the transfer in July 1994, No 482507 has just arrived at Bank. It has already lost the NSE sticker from the front end.
John Glover

Snow brings its own problems for the railway operator, especially when it freezes. Besides running rail adhesion difficulties, ice on the conductor rail will lead to arcing as the current collector shoes try to do their job. All is running well in February 1991, as a southbound 1959 stock train approaches East Finchley with a train for Morden via Charing Cross. However, the snow-covered lines to the centre platforms and the turnback siding indicate that they have negligible usage. *Martin Higginson*

A D stock train for Barking awaits departure from Wimbledon Platform 2 in January 1991. The platform edges have been cleared of snow, but this can be done only if there are staff available to do it. On the left of the picture, commuters for Waterloo on Platform 5 await their Network SouthEast service for Waterloo. The television screens which give the driver a view back along the whole train from his cab are clearly visible. *John Glover*

The days of the Jubilee Line 1983 stock are numbered, at least in their present guise. A southbound six-car formation for Charing Cross arrives at Queensbury in December 1996 with DM No 3760 of batch 2 of this stock leading. The Stanmore branch has changed 'ownership' twice. Originally a Metropolitan branch when it opened in 1932, it became part of the Bakerloo when that line was extended from Baker Street in 1939, and then part of the Jubilee when the opening of the Baker Street to Charing Cross link took place in 1979. *John Glover*

The new trains for the Jubilee Line Extension (and the rest of the line as well) are being built by GEC Alsthom at their Metro-Cammell factory at Washwood Heath. Here, a 1996 stock train, part of the batch of 59 six-car units, is seen on the company's test track. An additional 'special' trailer car may be added at a later date if required. The overhead catenary and lack of conductor rails is not a subtle hint that the trains are really destined for Birmingham's electrified suburban services! *GEC Alsthom*

The City & South London Railway took the view that a line which was entirely underground had no need of eye-level windows in the cars for the passengers. Consequently, the 'padded cells' as they quickly became known did have a certain resemblance to places at which one might be detained at Her Majesty's pleasure.

Internal width was a mere 6ft 10in, with a centre ceiling height of 7ft. This is coach No 30, built by the Ashbury Railway Carriage and Iron Co in 1890 and displayed at the London Transport Museum in Covent Garden. *Brian Morrison*

This view is of a 1992 Central Line stock car, which is certainly more generously dimensioned. The seating is all longitudinal, albeit with the centre pair of each group of six seats set back to allow greater standing capacity. Once again, there are no armrests, those fitted originally having proved unequal to the job. Public address announcements ('The next station is...' etc) are made by digitised speech as opposed to the shouts of a travelling conductor. *John Glover*

The Docklands Light Railway has provided a railway public transport link to the Isle of Dogs since the first section was opened in 1987. It has subsequently been extended, and had its capacity increased by resignalling as well as the provision of longer platforms. West India Quay, seen here in June 1994, is now a four-platformed station. A Class B90 BN car No 23 arrives at the front of a two-unit train, bound for Bank. Canary Wharf station is in the background. *John Glover*

In July 1994, Class P89 BREL car No 13 was dwarfed as it arrived from Stratford with a terminating train in the vast Canary Wharf station. These articulated twin units are 28.80m long. When the DLR was built, the first Canary Wharf station comprised single platforms on each side of a viaduct. It never opened and was later demolished. The present structure with its six platforms straddling three lines took its place some years later. *John Glover*

A train of silver District Line R stock, once the mainstay of that line's services, arrives at Acton Town with an eastbound train in May 1978. The characteristic flared edge to the lower body sides was introduced to prevent hopeful late arrivals jumping onto the footboards and holding on as the train accelerated away, while they prised the doors apart to gain entry to the saloon. With air doors, that approach does not work! Of note is the track walker, in those days without any form of high-visibility protective clothing. *John Glover*

Shoreditch was only an intermediate station until the link to Liverpool Street was severed. Later the terminus of the East London Line, it was reduced to a single platform, though the disused one had a commendable floral display in August 1969. Here, a train of clerestory-roofed Q stock arrives at journey's end. If the northern extension plans for the line come to fruition, Shoreditch station will be replaced, with the line taking a new alignment to raise it to the level of the disused portion of the North London Railway from north of Broad Street to Dalston. *Martin Higginson*

A C stock train, displaying some modest signs of graffiti, approaches Latimer Road with a Hammersmith-Whitechapel train in August 1990. The less than attractive image displayed was one of the key reasons that London Underground undertook an extensive refurbishment and updating programme on its rolling stock. Mid-life re-engineering became a reality, and with it a new corporate livery was applied. *John Glover*

C stock also forms this Wimbledon-Edgware Road District Line service in May 1990. This unit has been little defaced and has a much cleaner appearance. This is High Street Kensington; from this point, the Edgware Road trains have to form a joint service with the Circle Line. The constant joining and departing of services from the Circle on the various branches of the District, Metropolitan and Hammersmith & City is not perhaps the most sensible way to operate a service which has reliability as a goal, but an acceptable alternative service pattern has yet to be devised. *John Glover*

Two of the retired Q38 stock Driving Motor cars saw a new life for a time as surface stock pilot cars. These were used to ferry odd cars of rolling stock between depots as required. Formerly cars Nos 4416/7, they were renumbered L126 and L127 respectively and given the engineer's yellow livery when they were photographed at Acton Works in 1983. Later, they reverted to train red with original markings, and have since survived into preservation. *John Glover*

The Tunnel Cleaning Train, dating from the late 1970s, was fabricated at Acton Works from two withdrawn 1938 tube stock Driving Motors and new construction. A fan in the centre vehicle draws the dirt into the filter cars on either side, where it is stored for later disposal. This necessary but unglamorous vehicle was also pictured at Acton Works in 1983. *John Glover*

The 1972 tube stock, in both its MkI and MkII versions, was effectively a later version of the 1967 Victoria Line stock but without Automatic Train Operation (ATO) equipment and built for crew operation. Refurbished DM No 3239 in corporate livery leads a train of 1972 MkII stock out of Stonebridge Park Bakerloo Line depot, with a train for Elephant & Castle in May 1995. *John Glover*

A train of the very similar 1972 MkI stock arrives in
Morden Northern Line depot in November 1990,
carrying another of the experimental liveries. The
Northern Line has had the misfortune to be operated
by a mix of rolling stock types for many years, the
other main type being the 1959 tube stock built
originally for the Piccadilly Line. The 1995 tube
stock presently under construction will create a
standard fleet. *John Glover*

Dusk falls at Earl's Court in March 1989 as an eastbound D stock District Line train for Plaistow awaits departure. The external grab poles can be seen adjacent to some doors. These were fitted to help the mobility impaired to board and alight, but were removed subsequently due to attempts by young people to ride on the outside of the train. History never quite repeats itself... *John Glover*

The D stock trains have a mixture of transverse and longitudinal seating. The doors are single leaf, with passenger door opening control. This interior view shows the general arrangement of the 75 six-car trains, built in the early 1980s. They remain substantially as constructed, but the moquette does now appear a little dated. *John Glover*

Above:
This entrance to Bank station, with the Bank of England behind it, is at the junction of Poultry and Prince's Street. The style is similar to the other entrances and typical of its period — adequate, but not particularly inviting. It was photographed in December 1996. *John Glover*

Below:
The short Underground branch from Acton Town to South Acton met its probably inevitable demise as early as 28 February 1959. A week before closure, this was the scene at the entrance to South Acton station, which remains open today for North London Railways' services. *Author's collection*

Below:
A modest little station, West Finchley's ticket office was completely
reconstructed in the 1990s on the site used previously for a wooden building
with a passimeter-type ticket office in the middle. The latter dated from LNER
days. This picture was taken in August 1995. *John Glover*

Above:
Redolent still of the 1930s, this is the view from the drum-shaped ticket hall area of
St John's Wood station, which was opened on 20 November 1939. It is complete
still with the uplighters on the escalators, which themselves retain their wooden
treads. Unusually, daylight penetrates this normally totally enclosed area. This was
the view in December 1996. *John Glover*

The 1992 tube stock now monopolises Central Line services. An eastbound train with DM No 91245 in the lead arrives at North Acton Junction from the original Ealing Broadway branch. The later line to West Ruislip diverges here by means of a dive-under for westbound traffic. This line, opened in 1947/8, ran parallel to the Great Western's Birmingham main line, reduced over this section by the date of this picture in July 1994 to a little-used single track. How are the mighty fallen!
John Glover

At its eastern end, the Central Line reaches open country. Beyond Theydon Bois, an Epping-bound eight-car train traverses the green fields of Essex in the early evening of 4 May 1996. Spring was late that year, though the trees were just beginning to turn. Pastoral the scene may be, but the parallel M11 is only just out of sight over the hill beyond the line, while the M25 crosses the railway a short distance further north and before Epping is reached. *Martin Higginson*

The venerable 1938 tube stock lives on in small numbers on the Isle of Wight, where the trains are now owned by Eversholt Holdings and operated by Island Line TOC. With No 483007 leading, a two-unit train runs the length of Ryde Pier from

Ryde Esplanade station, the town stretching out behind it in July 1992.
John Glover

Later that same day, the Class 483 set is seen north of Brading and again heading for Ryde Pier Head on the section thence to Smallbrook Junction. The railway is now single track from Sandown right through to beyond Smallbrook, a distance of over four miles. With a running time of 10min or so for this section, given a maximum permitted speed of 45mph, this and other line restrictions do limit the ability to run frequent services. *John Glover*

The choice by London Transport of perpetuating steam traction for engineering duties on the Underground was one of those curious turns of history, as a result of which steam outlived that on the big railway next door by nearly three years. The last steam operation was on 6 June 1971. This picture of ex-Great Western 0-6-0 pannier tank L95 (formerly BR No 5764) was taken at Neasden shed in September 1969. *Martin Higginson*

Of the 13 ex-GW 0-6-0PTs owned from time to time by London Transport, many survived into preservation. L99 (formerly BR No 7715) was built by Kerr Stuart in 1930 and was the last to be acquired for use on the Underground, in June 1963. Withdrawn in January 1970, it is now resident at Quainton Road, Buckinghamshire, where it was seen in April 1993 passing 'E' class Metropolitan 0-4-4T No 1 of 1898. This latter locomotive previously carried service stock No L44, as which it was withdrawn in March 1964. *Brian Morrison*

The Northern Line's extension north of Golders Green was delayed, to the extent that when building commenced a number of new houses had to be demolished to accommodate the railway viaduct. The road was stopped up and became two dead ends. A southbound 1959 stock train, from Edgware to Kennington via Charing Cross, passes the scene of long-ago despoliation in June 1990. Brent Cross station can be seen in the distance. *John Glover*

Leytonstone is where the Hainault loop of the Central Line joins the original Great Eastern line to Epping. From here to Newbury Park the loop line is in tunnel, and in this May 1990 picture a westbound Hainault to Ealing Broadway train of 1962 stock is joining the main line. To the left of the picture, an eastbound train descends. The catch point on the right, protecting the tunnel entrance, seems to be of an impossibly tight radius. However, its purpose is to derail a train to prevent a head-on collision should it be required so to do. *John Glover*

The British Transport Museum at Clapham in an old bus garage was eventually closed and the collections dispersed to the new National Railway Museum at York and to Syon Park for the LT exhibits. In September 1970, the Metropolitan Railway 'A' class 4-4-0T built by Beyer Peacock in 1866 was pictured at Clapham. These locomotives worked all the principal Metropolitan services, with considerable success, while similar locomotives were acquired by the District Railway. Despite rapid progress with electrification, this hardy warrior lasted in service stock (where it had the number L45) until 1948. It was then withdrawn for official preservation. *John Glover*

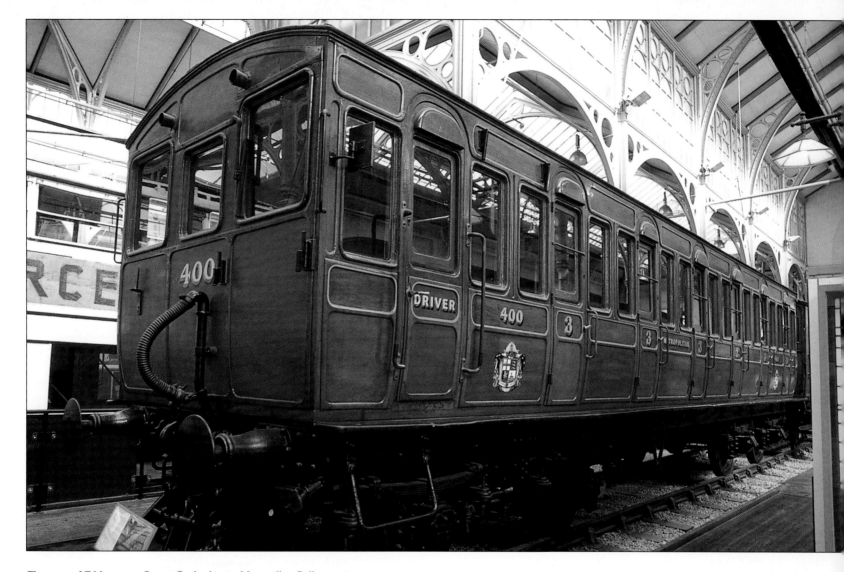

The present LT Museum at Covent Garden houses Metropolitan Railway steam
stock No 400. This vehicle has had a varied career, having been converted from
steam stock to an electric Control Trailer in 1921 and then back again 20 years later
to work the Chesham shuttle. *John Glover*

Bounds Green on the Piccadilly northern push beyond Finsbury Park was opened to traffic on 19 September 1932. Described unflatteringly as 'a box with chopped off corners and a ventilation tower', this was perhaps not the most inspiring of the stations of its era. Nevertheless, it draws attention to itself much more effectively than a hole in the wall — or a hole in the pavement. People must be able to see and recognise the Underground product, helped as always by the display of the roundel. The station was photographed in July 1989. *John Glover*

Above:
Newbury Park station at platform level is pure Great Eastern, but at street level this huge arched roof was constructed to accommodate double-deck buses serving the station. It earned its creator, Oliver Hill, the Festival of Britain award for architectural merit in 1951. Seen here in December 1996, devoid of bus services, one might remark that it is a little draughty for waiting passenger in this open location alongside the A12 Eastern Avenue. The station opened for Central Line services on 14 December 1947. *John Glover*

Right:
The roundel, Newbury Park style, is displayed in such a way that it cannot be missed by those approaching. This photograph was taken in December 1996. *John Glover*

The date 13 September 1989 marked a formal launch at Acton Works of the London Underground rolling stock refurbishment scheme. In each case, substantial interior changes have been carried out, as well as more basic maintenance requirements. Pictured here, from left to right, are three Driving Motor vehicles. They are Metropolitan Line A62 stock DM No 5132, Victoria Line 1967 stock DM No 3010 and Hammersmith & City/Circle and Edgware Road-Wimbledon C77 stock DM No 5585. *Brian Morrison*

A car for the new Jubilee Line trains was seen at the Railtech exhibition at Wembley in 1996. Displaying somewhat unusual destination information, the 1996 stock DM demonstrates the appearance of the 21st-century Underground tube train.
Brian Morrison

Boston Manor, Piccadilly Line, sees a 1973 stock train for Cockfosters approaching on an eastbound working in August 1990. In anticipation of the needs of airline passengers and their associated luggage, the 1973 stock was built with greater standbacks inside the door areas to provide a place to put luggage. In practice, though, most passengers are determined to keep their luggage as close to hand as possible — especially on a 45min or so journey between Heathrow and central London. *John Glover*

Above:
An early attempt to upgrade the 1973 stock resulted in one three-car unit being painted with red train ends and passenger doors, instead of the corporate red now used. Each of the vehicles also received a new interior layout. It is seen here in May 1995 approaching Barons Court station on a Heathrow working, shortly after leaving the long tunnel section from Arnos Grove. *John Glover*

Right:
In June 1996, the first of the Piccadilly Line trains to the finally agreed refurbishment programme was pictured approaching Northfields on an eastbound working to Cockfosters. Internally, an all-longitudinal seating arrangement has been used. The all-red front has been superseded by a black and red design, as seen also on the 1992 ADtranz stock and the 1995 and 1996 GEC Alsthom stocks. *Brian Morrison*

Woodside Park is a Great Northern Railway station, which still boasts two signalboxes! Both had been disused for years and were downgraded to useful huts for putting things in. The Underground 'stile' for staff to cross the cable runs may be noted. The former goods yard on the right of the picture is now the station car park.

In this May 1988 picture, a train of the experimental 1956 stock, forerunner of the 1959 stock, leaves on a northbound train for High Barnet having run via Bank. This is the Metro-Cammell train, with car No 1003 bringing up the rear. *John Glover*

Above:
The Cravens Co of Sheffield built the 1960 stock in the hope that this would be the design adopted for the Central Line to replace the pre-1938 standard stock then in use. But it was not to be, the order remaining at 12 Driving Motor cars only. The intermediate trailers were converted for use from other stock. In the event, the 1959 stock was multiplied as the very similar 1962 stock for the Central. Here, a surviving pair of 1960 trains on the Woodford-Hainault shuttle cross at Chigwell in June 1990. The approaching train is for Woodford and a 1938 stock trailer can be seen as the centre vehicle.
John Glover

Right:
A 1960 stock train was latterly painted red, a livery which the DMs never carried as the bodies were built from unpainted aluminium. It is seen here in Hainault depot sidings on the same day.
John Glover

The time is 02.01 on 31 July 1990. The place is St James's Park, eastbound platform, and the train the 00.39 engineer's special from Neasden to Upminster. Metropolitan 0-4-4T locomotive No 1 heads a couple of ex-BR coaches, a MkI BSK and a MkII FO. Battery locomotive L44 discreetly brings up the rear. The dot matrix indicator confirms that the train is 'not in service'. *Brian Morrison*

The battery locomotive which piloted the train was then reattached and the train moved forward so that L44, with cab light on, could also be pictured in the then new engineer's livery. L44 was one of the batch built by the then BREL at Doncaster in the mid-1970s. Its diminutive tube gauge size is most noticeable, especially alongside the BR coaching stock. *Brian Morrison*

A pair of the TransPlant fleet of battery locomotives, L51 and L44. Both are from the batch built by BREL Doncaster in 1973/4 and sport the TransPlant livery. They were photographed at Ruislip depot on 15 March 1997. The battery fleet are built to tube gauge, which provides them with sufficient clearance to operate throughout the system. *John Glover*

Six railway tracks cross Kilburn High Road at a crossroads, with an approximately 45° angle. Into this is incorporated a Jubilee Line island platform station. Surprisingly, the result at street level is far from oppressive. The bridge bearing the southbound Jubilee and Metropolitan tracks (an A stock train can just be seen) carries a message which leaves observers in no doubt as to its one-time owners. *John Glover*

53

This interior view is of 1983 stock of the batch 1 version. It was photographed in December 1996. These trains were the only tube stock to have been fitted with single sliding doors throughout; in this they bear close resemblance to the D surface stock trains which just preceded them. However, loading and unloading of passengers has proved to be relatively slow, and was one reason for not incorporating some of these vehicles in the new rolling stock order which became the 1996 stock fleet. *John Glover*

In December 1996, a 1983 stock train heading north for Stanmore approaches Willesden Green. The tracks on the right are those of the Great Central route, on which the passenger services of Chiltern Railways run to the junction at Neasden and thence either to Aylesbury or to Banbury and Birmingham Snow Hill. *John Glover*

A 1967 Victoria Line train emerges from Grange Hill tunnel with a Woodford-Hainault service. With this line equipped to Automatic Train Operation as a precursor to the Victoria Line installation for the opening progressively of the latter from 1968 to 1972, the 1967 stock trains were able to work here. This was useful for initial testing and equipment familiarisation, and was used on occasion subsequently as here in September 1983. *John Glover*

This 1986 view shows how attractive a pristine aluminium-bodied and unpainted train can look. This 1967 Victoria Line train is arriving at Northumberland Park depot on the link from Seven Sisters; this is the only part of the line on the surface. It runs here alongside Railtrack's Lea Valley line for a short distance. Local authorities have on several occasions explored the idea of a Victoria Line branch to Northumberland Park and beyond. *John Glover*

Standard stock in Rail Blue, albeit with grey doors, is seen at Ryde Pier Head in August 1980. On the left is 4-VEC unit No 045 with the IOW tail disk in lieu of the oil tail lamp; on the right is 3-TIS unit No 032. Each would have formed part of a seven-coach train. The platforms here once had four faces as can be seen by the positions of the canopies, which have not changed. In the foreground is the remains of the pier tramway track. *John Glover*

Sandown had a signalbox with a commanding view of the station area. No 485041
in Network SouthEast livery arrives in July 1988 with a down train for Shanklin,
crossing an up train which has recently vacated the single line stub.
John Glover

East Finchley station of 1939 exhibits some of the rounded features associated with the 'Odeon' style; it was a very extensive rebuild of the GNR station for the electrification and transfer to London Transport. The centre lines on Platforms 3 (left) and 2 (right) remain disused, except for setting down or picking up passenger from trains en route to or from Highgate depot. Consideration has been given to making the centre lines into loops which can be accessed by trains proceeding to or from Archway. This view, looking south, was taken in August 1995. *John Glover*

An occasion was staged on the centre lines at East Finchley to demonstrate the benefits of stock refurbishment. The date was 19 July 1990. On the right is a 1972 MkI train, which visitors were asked to compare with the 1959 stock train, painted up in 'heritage' livery. *Brian Morrison*

Finchley Central Northern Line station had changed little over the years, seen here with a 1938 stock train arriving from High Barnet with a service to Kennington via Charing Cross in August 1976. The three-platformed layout is to accommodate the Mill Hill East services at the platform on the far left, which serves also to provide cross-platform connections on occasion. Had World War 2 not intervened, Finchley Central was to have been rebuilt as a four-platformed station, but work on this project never commenced. *John Glover*

SITE OF THE WORST CIVILIAN DISASTER
OF THE SECOND WORLD WAR

IN MEMORY OF
173 MEN, WOMEN AND CHILDREN
WHO LOST THEIR LIVES ON THE
EVENING OF WEDNESDAY 3RD MARCH 1943
DESCENDING THESE STEPS TO BETHNAL GREEN
UNDERGROUND AIR RAID SHELTER

NOT FORGOTTEN

At Hammersmith H&C Line station in June 1995, the barrier is still manned. Beyond, a C stock train awaits departure. This picture demonstrates that presenting a clean and cheerful appearance to the customers does not necessarily involve the spending of large sums of money. *John Glover*

Above:
In November 1992, the revamping of the Great Western main line out of Paddington
in preparation for electrification for the Heathrow Express was well under way.
A refurbished C stock emerges from the Underground's Subway Tunnel beneath the
main line on an eastbound service to Whitechapel. *Brian Morrison*

Right:
The interior of the refurbished C stock has substituted longitudinal seating for
transverse sets of four, while retaining the same seating capacity. The cars have also
had new windows cut into the end bulkheads to create visibility throughout the
train, to enhance perceptions of personal safety. One side effect has been the
increased use of plain-clothes ticket inspectors, since the approach of the uniformed
variety becomes much more obvious. This photograph was taken in December
1996. *John Glover*

The Beckton branch of the Docklands Light Railway incorporates some running in the central reservation of the Docklands Spine Road, with the DLR diving down below at roundabouts to stations at both Cyprus and Beckton Park. In July 1994,

Class B92 DLR car No 81, which was SELTRAC signalling equipped from new, descends into Beckton Park station with a train from the temporary terminus at Poplar to Beckton. *John Glover*

DLR car No 52 calls at the futuristic Royal Victoria station with a Poplar-Beckton service in July 1994. Sadly, passengers are noticeable by their absence. On the right are the lines of the Railtrack North Woolwich branch; in the background, both begin the sweep round to Canning Town. Each is electrified by its own (incompatible) version of dc third rail. *John Glover*

On Christmas Eve 1996, a D stock train arrives at the former London, Tilbury & Southend station of Plaistow, bound for Upminster. The main line platforms here still exist, but have been disused for many years. This and the other stations on the District Line from Bromley-by-Bow eastwards (excepting only Barking and Upminster) passed to London Undergound control nearly 30 years ago. *John Glover*

The A stock trains are already approaching 40 years in service, and might be expected to soldier on for another decade or so. A rather old-fashioned appearance pervades the Watford-bound service, seen here as it approaches Neasden in May 1988. Should the Metropolitan Line's Croxley link to Watford Junction ever be built, it is a fair guess that it will be an A stock train that makes the first journey across it. *John Glover*

In September 1994, a 1962 tube stock train arrives in the middle platform at White City with a westbound train for Ealing Broadway. In over 30 years of monopolising Central Line services, these units have acquitted themselves well, but latterly were showing their age. *John Glover*

The 1972 MkII stock brought some relief to the aluminium colour scheme of the Underground in the 1970s and 1980s with its red doors. In the author's opinion, this was one of the more successful treatments. A Harrow & Wealdstone to Elephant & Castle service leaves Willesden Junction in July 1994, amid detritus which suggests that the different lines in the picture are electrified with fourth rail, third rail, or not at all. *John Glover*

On the Isle of Wight, No 483005 runs off the 700yd pier into Ryde Esplanade station in May 1992, with a train to Shanklin. The train may be familiar in shape and general appearance, though somehow even ex-Underground trains do not look quite right on a pier! *John Glover*

Internally, though, there is no doubt as to their origins. This is DMSO(A) No 127 from 1938 stock set No 483007. The guard's door panels are retained, as indeed is the pair of tip-up seats. Strip lighting has been installed to replace tungsten, and there are no longer any hand grips hanging from the ceiling. *John Glover*

The new trains for the Northern Line are being supplied in an entirely new form of contract. GEC Alsthom will be responsible for maintaining the trains and supplying sufficient numbers to LUL to operate the service on a daily rental basis. The contract is for a 20-year agreement and is performance related. Depot staff have transferred to GEC Alsthom. This picture shows one of the new 1995 stock trains under construction at the Metro-Cammell plant in Washwood Heath. *GEC Alsthom*

A total of 106 six-car trains of 1995 tube stock is to be supplied to undertake the Northern Line contract; this picture shows one of the first trains to arrive on London metals. DM No 51501 was photographed at Ruislip on 15 March 1997. Work on strengthened power supplies, signalling renewal and a general upgrading of track quality will be needed to take full advantage of the new equipment, especially if overall journey times are to be reduced. *John Glover*

The best of the Standard stock cars were retrieved from the Isle of Wight; together with former LUL personnel carrier conversions, it is hoped that one day these may be returned into working order. The ensemble is seen here at Upminster depot in September 1991 with a DM from No 485041 at the near end. *Brian Morrison*

Above:
No 12, *Sarah Siddons*, is the Metropolitan electric locomotive built by Metropolitan Vickers in 1922. Still maintained as part of the engineering fleet as a Brake Block Test Locomotive, *Sarah* sees use on special trains. Here she is seen passing Moor Park with a train of BR MkII air-conditioned coaches, en route for Watford. *John Glover*

Right:
The plaque below the nameplate reads: 'In August 1975 this locomotive took part in the exhibition and cavalcade to commemorate the 150th anniversary of the Stockton & Darlington Railway'. *John Glover*

Left:
In December 1996, an A60 stock train for Baker Street headed by DM No 5056 in corporate livery approaches Neasden at speed on the southbound Metropolitan Line. The overbridge carries the A406 North Circular Road. The A60/A62 stock monopolises all Metropolitan main line services. In summary, this means all services beyond Wembley Park, if one excludes the few Piccadilly Line workings from Rayners Lane to Uxbridge. *John Glover*

At Queen's Park in December 1996, a pair of 1972 MkII trains occupy the two roads of the south shed. DM No 3344 on the left and DM No 3357 on the right are surrounded by railways. From the left, these are: the up dc local line to Euston (which has an over-run for the fourth rail), the southbound and northbound Bakerloo Line tracks, the down dc local line from Euston and the West Coast main line. *John Glover*

79

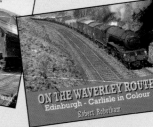